HENR Great Adventure
TALES FROM THE CLEARING BOOK 1

WHAT PEOPLE ARE SAYING ...

Luann Hamill has woven a gentle and delightful narrative where children discover the truth that books can transport them anywhere, allow them to be anything, and experience great adventures without ever leaving home. A wonderful tool to help parents develop a life-long thirst for reading in their child.
—**Mary Mueller**, Author, *What Did You Bring Me?*

Henry's Great Adventure is a delightful blend of playfulness and wisdom. Henry the turtle and his two friends—the rabbit and the owl—help us see that reading books can take us on all kinds of wonderful adventures. The playful rhymes and winsome illustrations will make this book a favorite of children and their parents alike.
—**Ken Wilson**, author of *Loved More Than You Know*

HENRY'S
Great Adventure

TALES FROM THE CLEARING BOOK 1

LUANN HAMILL
ILLUSTRATED BY NATHALIE LEWIS

Copyright Notice

Henry's Great Adventure, Tales From the Clearing, Book 1

First edition. Copyright © 2020 by Luann Hamill The information contained in this book is the intellectual property of Luann Hamill and is governed by United States and International copyright laws. All rights reserved. No part of this publication, either text or image, may be used for any purpose other than personal use. Therefore, reproduction, modification, storage in a retrieval system, or retransmission, in any form or by any means, electronic, mechanical, or otherwise, for reasons other than personal use, except for brief quotations for reviews or articles and promotions, is strictly prohibited without prior written permission by the publisher.

Cover Design: Nathalie Lewis, Derinda Babcock

Interior Design: Derinda Babcock

Editor(s): Derinda Babcock, Deb Haggerty

Illustrated by: Nathalie Lewis

Library Cataloging Data

Names: Hamill, Luann (Luann Hamill)

Henry's Great Adventure, Tales From the Clearing Book 1 / Luann Hamill

46 p. 21.6 cm × 21.6 cm (8.5 in × 8.5 in.)

Description: Henry the turtle wakes up one morning in the place he loves most in the world—his home, his Wonder Place. But on this particular morning, all he can think about is leaving his Wonder Place to have an adventure, like the ones he reads about in his beloved books. Where will his journey take him? What will he find? Go with him and find out.

Identifiers: ISBN-13: 978-1-951970-35-2 (paperback) | 978-1-951970-36-9 (trade hardcover) | 978-1-951970-37-6 (trade paperback) | 978-1-951970-38-3 (e-book)

Key Words: Children, ages 4 to 8, Picture book, Rhyming, Adventures, Reading, Animals

LCCN: 2020936394 Fiction

AUTHOR'S DEDICATION

For Tom,
who I have loved as long as I can remember remembering

ILLUSTRATOR'S DEDICATION

To my two redhead muses.
You make everyday an adventure.

Henry the turtle just loved to read books
About heroes' adventures—the courage this took.
One day he awoke with a thought in his head,
What if *he* had his own adventure instead?

He tidied his Wonder Place—made it look spiffy
Then packed up his favorite things in a jiffy.
Apples and brittle when he needed a bite,
And for when it got dark, his firefly light.

Henry was sad to be leaving his home,
But he wanted an adventure he could call his own.
His little legs carried him down a path in the woods
Moving slowly, so slowly, the one way he could.

After a while, he stopped for a snack.
He thought about home and turned to go back.
But then he heard something from just up ahead
And followed the path to a clearing instead.

In the shade of the forest lay a large fallen tree.
He was curious but scared, so he moved carefully.
Sitting on the log was a pretty brown rabbit
Putting flowers in a teacup, which seemed a strange habit.

As Henry approached, the rabbit looked up
And carefully lowered her tiny teacup.
"My name is Violet, and this is our home.
Oh, I see you brought books! We have some of our own."

"My name is Henry," he said with a smile,
"And I have been traveling for such a long while."
"Rocco the owl lives with me too.
He told me last night he dreamt about you."

Violet invited Henry inside
And slid off the log in one smooth slide.
Could this be my adventure? He gave this a thought.
When he followed her inside, what a surprise he got!

Sitting in the middle of a very large bed
Blinked a wise looking hooty owl 'neath a blanket of red.
"Welcome, Henry, we're so glad you're here,"
And he quietly motioned Henry to come near.

"Do you like to read?" Henry said to the pair.

"Yes," Rocco answered, "We like books in our lair."

"But books are just reading," Henry offered politely.

"I want an adventure," he explained to them brightly.

"Henry, you're wrong." Rocco shook his wise head.

He invited Henry to sit on the bed.

Rocco explained that the stories they read

Become their own stories, and Violet agreed.

"Violet," he said, "will you please choose a book?"
Henry moved closer for a much better look.
The one that she chose was called *Tales From The Sea,*
And they all chose a character they wanted to be.

Henry chose the hero with the gleaming gold sword,
Defending his ship from the pirates on board.
They acted their parts and became so excited
Henry fell off the bed and Rocco laughed—delighted!

"Do you see what we mean?" Rocco finally said,
And Violet helped Henry climb back on the bed.
"I certainly do," Henry said with a thrill,
"I'll remember this always, I promise I will."

"I don't have to leave my Wonder Place at all!"
And he looked all around him and up at the walls.
Books were piled high from the ceiling to the floor
And everywhere he looked, he saw many more.

"You've had lots of adventures from what I can see,"
And they all laughed together quite happily.
The three were now friends, to that they agreed,
And soon the time came for Henry to leave.

"Thank you, Rocco, for opening my eyes.
I've had more adventures than I realized."
"My pleasure, dear Henry, come back any day,
And please visit often, as you now know the way."

Henry said his goodbyes with a promise to return.
He couldn't wait to get home after all that he'd learned.
So, he made his way slowly, back through the wood,
As slowly was surely the one way he could.

ABOUT THE AUTHOR

Luann has always loved writing, but rhyming is her favorite writing style. Aside from writing custom pieces for family, friends, and gifting, she has also written two rhyming books currently available on Amazon: *The Tale Of Static Kitty* and *Monkeys In The Fridge*. She is very excited to be unveiling the first book in her Tales From the Clearing collection, *Henry's Great Adventure*. Luann makes her home in Plymouth, Massachusetts, with her high school sweetheart, Tom, her two daughters, Missy and Jess, and two dogs, Myles and Marty.

ABOUT THE ILLUSTRATOR

Nathalie Lewis earned a bachelor of fine arts degree from Laval University in Quebec, Canada. She went on to pursue advanced studies in Anthropology and worked in Archeology for the city of Quebec for several years. She is now an artist and an occasional freelance illustrator. Nathalie illustrated an educational graphic novel which won the Independent Publisher book award for excellence. Nathalie now lives in New England with her family.

Made in the USA
Monee, IL
04 May 2020